I Love Being My Own Autistic Self

A thAutoons Book

Written and Illustrated by

Landon Bryce

For the autistic people and their families
who teach and inspire me every day by being part
of the thAutcast community.

I would like to thank the following people,
who made invaluable suggestions on this book:

Jennifer Sheridan
Karla Fisher
Paula C. Durbin-Westby
Amy Sequenzia
Adam Bailey
Tina Jones
Tasia Markoff

Hi! My name is Vector, and I'm autistic.

It's hard to explain what autism is, partly because autistic people are so different from each other.

Some people say autism is a disability.

Some people say it's a difference.

I think it's both.

There are some good things about my autism:

I have interesting and unusual ideas about things.

I'm very observant and I often notice things that other people don't.

I'm very honest. I like to know the rules for every situation, and I like it when everybody follows them. It doesn't usually occur to me to try to take advantage of other people.

My autism makes it easy for me to learn about and remember some kinds of things.

I am able to focus very intensely on the things I like.

There are some bad things about my autism:

It makes it hard for me to communicate.

Some things are very difficult for me to learn.

I don't have very precise physical coordination. I don't always know when I am hungry or tired.

I am often very anxious. It's hard for me to relax and feel like things are okay. I'm scared a lot of the time.

I find unexpected changes very upsetting. A lot of the time, I prefer to do things the same way over and over.

Some of the things I like and dislike are unusual, and it can be hard for me to find people who share my interests.

My senses are easily overwhelmed. Bright lights give me headaches. Loud noises make me jumpy. Strong smells make me sick to my stomach. Any strong sensation can make it impossible for me to concentrate on anything else.

I also experience some sensations less intensely than most people do.

Sometimes it makes people uncomfortable when I talk about the good parts of my autism.

They might think I am saying that autistic people are better than other people, but being proud of who I am does not mean I think other people are worse than me. They might think I am saying that I don't think autistic people need support or treatment, but I think those can be good things.

Mostly, they might think that I am saying that autism is only a good thing, and that I am not being considerate of people whose autism causes them a lot of problems.

But, even though I'm proud of being autistic, autism is very hard for me, and I know it can be even harder for other people.

Sometimes people get angry with me when I talk about the parts of my autism that are hard for me. It hurts their feelings, and they worry that I am giving people negative ideas about what it means to be autistic.

But I think the only way that autistic people can help each other with the parts of our lives that are painful is if we talk about them sometimes.

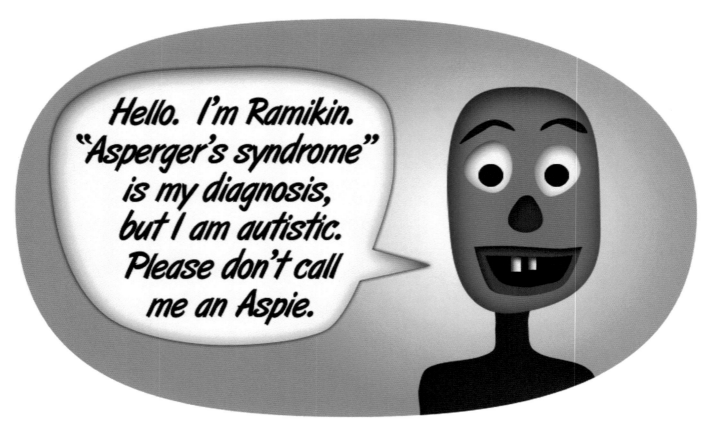

This is my friend Ramikin, and she is also autistic. The kind of autism she has is called Asperger's syndrome, but she does not like to use those words. She likes to say she is autistic.

The kind of autism I have is called pervasive developmental disorder not otherwise specified, or PDD-NOS, for short. I also like to say that I am autistic.

This is a good thing because doctors are probably going to stop diagnosing people with Asperger's syndrome and PDD-NOS soon. Instead, we will all have Autism Spectrum Disorder (ASD).

Although Ramikin and I are both autistic, we are very different from each other. I like to go outside in the sun and walk for hours, but the sun makes Ramikin feel sick. She likes to spend hours talking to her friends on the telephone, but I would never use the telephone if I did not have to.

To make things even more confusing, other people with Aspergers or PDD-NOS are not different from each other in the same ways that Ramikin and I are. Ramikin has a hard time with eye contact, but not everyone with Aspergers has that problem. She does not like to be called an Aspie, but some other autistic people do.

Ramikin and I both have a hard time understanding how other people are feeling by looking at their faces and observing the way they act.

For me, it's also difficult to get along with other people. They sometimes think I'm rude because I am usually very direct. I don't understand why people like to ask "How are you?" when they aren't interested in the answer.

Ramikin finds things like that much easier than I do.

Or maybe it's less that those things are easier for Ramikin than it is that she works harder at them than I do. I know that sometimes being around other people is so hard for me that I don't try as hard as I should to be pleasant to be around.

Ramikin is almost always polite to other people.

Some autistic people are. Others aren't. We're real people, just like everyone else.

Okay... so maybe sometimes I'm obnoxious AND autistic.

This is my best friend, Marko. Marko has classic autism, or Kanner's autism.

He does not talk.

He may have intellectual challenges that go beyond his difficulties with language. And he may not.

It seems to be very difficult for him to learn new things, but it may be more that it's hard for him to show other people what he knows.

I love spending time with Marko. He's the person I know who is most like me. We like listening to music together and taking walks.

My other best friend is my dog. Some autistic people find it easier to relate to animals than other people. But not all autistic people are like that. Some are scared of dogs. Ramikin just doesn't like them.

Like I said before, it's hard to understand autism because autistic people are so different from each other.

This is my friend Pang. Pang is neurotypical, which means that she doesn't have autism.

It's hard for Pang and me to understand each other.

Sometimes we say things that hurt each other's feelings.

Some neurotypical people don't understand that seeming normal is hard work for autistic people like me—such hard work that it might not be worth the effort.

One thing that is hard for Pang to understand is stimming. Stimming is "self-stimulating behavior"—things autistic people do over and over in order to calm down or feel better.

I flap my hands. Sometimes I rock back and forth. Other autistic people do other things, like humming or chewing gum. Neurotypical people stim, too. It's a very common way for people to decrease anxiety.

I know that my stimming can make other people nervous because it is unusual to be around and it can be distracting. I try to be considerate. But it takes a lot of work and energy for me not to stim at all. I wish more people were comfortable with it.

I like myself the way I am. I don't like to have to pretend to be different in order to fit in. Sometimes I do need to, but I'm not happy about it.

This is my sister Manta. Manta is also neurotypical. We love each other very much, but we disagree almost all the time.

We especially disagree about autism.

It's been very hard for Manta to have an autistic brother. I got more attention than she did when we were little, and she had to take on many responsibilities when she was young.

One thing I love about Manta is that she works very hard to try to help autistic people and their families.

One thing we disagree about is the way that she does it. She thinks the best way to help autistic people is to help us be as much like neurotypical people as possible.

I think the best way to help autistic people is to help us be happy and useful.

Manta likes to tell people that autism is a crisis or an epidemic. Those things hurt my feelings. They also make other people afraid of me, which makes it harder for me to find work or make friends.

Another thing we disagree about is what to call people like me. Manta doesn't like it when I call myself autistic. She wants me to say "person with autism" instead.

My sister has very kind reasons for that. She wants people to see me as a person first, and she wants them to care about and value me as an individual. Sometimes people look at people like me and think that the label "autism" is all there is to us. Manta wants people to think about things I can do, not just my disability.

But I like to call myself autistic. To say "with autism" feels to me like I'm trying to separate myself from something that is a very important part of who I am, the good parts and the bad parts.

Manta's friend Dr. Chip is a scientist who studies autism. I know he wants to help people like me, but sometimes he says things that hurt my feelings.

Some of the things that he says about autistic people are true about me and some of the other autistic people I know. But almost none of the things he says apply to all of the autistic people I know, and some of the things he says don't seem to be true at all.

It makes me especially sad when Manta and Dr. Chip talk about "autism prevention." I am glad I was born, and I'm proud to be who I am. I love my autistic friends. I think keeping people like Marko and Ramikin and me from being born would be very sad.

I get frustrated because Manta and Dr. Chip talk a lot about what to do about autism, but they don't like to include any autistic people in the conversation. They don't mind if I listen and nod my head when they talk.

But if I start to express my own opinions, and they are different from theirs, they get angry and they stop listening. Sometimes they say that I don't really understand what they are talking about because my autism limits my understanding.

Sometimes they say that they are really talking about people who are much more disabled by autism than I am, so I can't understand how hard their lives are.

But I know their lives are hard.

And I know that autism makes my life hard in ways that are hard for them to understand.

I think I understand autism better than they do because I have it.

I think we can help people like my friend Marko by listening to them, paying attention to the things they say without using words, and helping them learn how to express themselves in ways that are easier for us to understand.

I think we need to accept everyone for who they are in order to really help them.

I want Marko's life to be easier, but I want it to be his life.

My autistic friends and I are very different from our neurotypical friends.

We are also very different from each other.

But, as different as we are, we can all learn to be friends.

We all make contributions to the world.

We're all equally human.

And we can all learn to love each other and ourselves, exactly as we are.

Made in the USA
Lexington, KY
26 August 2013